RIDLEY, Sarah

Life in Roman
times

EVERYDAY HISTORY

LIFE IN

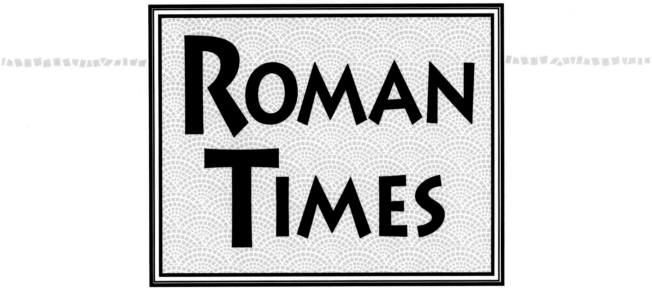

ROMAN TIMES

SARAH RIDLEY

W
FRANKLIN WATTS
LONDON•SYDNEY

First published in 2007
by Franklin Watts

Copyright © Franklin Watts 2007

Franklin Watts
338 Euston Road
London NW1 3BH

Franklin Watts Australia
Level 17/207 Kent Street
Sydney, NSW 2000

A CIP catalogue record for this book is available from the British Library.

ISBN 978 0 7496 7803 6

Printed in China

Franklin Watts is a division of
Hachette Children's Books, an Hachette Livre UK company.

The text of this book is based on
Clues to the Past – Everyday Life in Roman Times
by Mike Corbishley
Copyright © Franklin Watts 1993

Picture credits:
Ancient Art and Architecture Collection: 7b, 18t, 20t, 25b.
Courtesy of the Trustees of the British Museum: front cover br, 7t, 8t, 10t, 22t, 26t.
Colchester Museums: 24t.
Mike Corbishley: 6t.
Michael Holford: front cover bl, 6c, 16t (both), 28t.
Museum of London: front cover tr, 6b.
Vinolanda Trust 14t.
Roger White: 12t.
Reproduced by Courtesy of the Yorkshire Museum/Woodmansterne: 5t, 30t.

CONTENTS

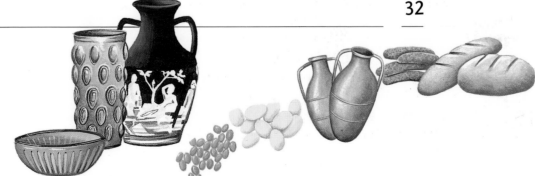

WHO WERE THE ROMANS?

Two thousand years ago, the Romans were the most powerful nation in Europe and around the Mediterranean Sea. About 60 million people lived in their empire. The official language of all these people was Latin but they spoke their own languages as well – such as Celtic and ancient Greek.

The Roman Empire began when the tribe, known as the *Latins*, took over the city of Rome in Italy. They began to conquer the lands around them and became known as the Romans. Wherever they went, they built towns and introduced Roman life.

Roman coins

This map (*right*) shows the Roman Empire about 1800 years ago.

BRITANNIA

LUGDUNENS[E] GALLIA

AQUITAN[IA]

ATLANTIC OCEAN

NAR[B]

TARRACONENSIS

LUSITANIA

BAETICA

MAURET[ANIA] CEASARIE[NSIS]

MAURETANIA TINGITANA

SOME IMPORTANT DATES FROM ROMAN TIMES

800–400 BCE

753 Legend says Rome was founded by Romulus.

400–100 BCE

264–241 First Punic War against the Carthaginians.
218–201 Second Punic War. Hannibal crosses the Alps by elephant to attack the Romans.
149–146 Final Punic War – Carthaginians defeated.

100 BCE–0 CE

58–49 Julius Caesar conquers Gaul (France) and invades Britain.
27 Augustus becomes Rome's first emperor.

0–100 CE

14 Emperor Augustus dies.
43 The Romans conquer Britain.
79 Mount Vesuvius in Italy erupts and the cities of Pompeii and Herculaneum are destroyed.

WHAT DID THE ROMANS LOOK LIKE?

Some portraits and statues of Roman people survive. They show that Roman people looked different all around the Empire.

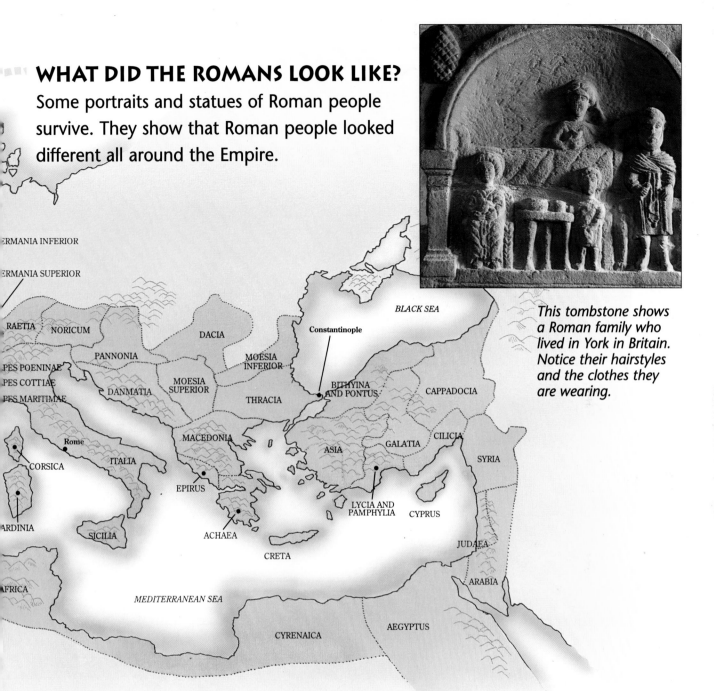

This tombstone shows a Roman family who lived in York in Britain. Notice their hairstyles and the clothes they are wearing.

100–200 CE

122 Emperor Hadrian rules. Hadrian's Wall is begun in northern Britain.

200–300 CE

212 All free men are made Roman citizens.
284 The Roman Empire is divided into two parts – east and west.

300–400 CE

312 Emperor Constantine rules. He founds a new capital city in the east, Constantinople.
367 Britain is attacked by "barbarians".

400–600 CE

409 German armies attack Rome.
476 The last Roman emperor is overthrown and the western Empire collapses.

HOW DO WE KNOW ABOUT THE ROMANS?

Detectives look for clues to help them solve crimes. Archaeologists and historians call their clues to the past "evidence". We can find out about the Romans from three sorts of evidence – the clues discovered by archaeologists, buildings that are still standing today and Roman writings.

(Above) Archaeologists carefully excavate a Roman site. (Below) This Roman mosaic gives us information about how the Romans harvested grapes and made wine.

ARCHAEOLOGICAL EVIDENCE

What do you think happens to the things you throw away? When your dustbin is emptied, some things rot away quickly, like paper and food. Other materials take longer, like fabric and wood, and some never rot, like glass and some metals. In the same way, only some objects survive from Roman times. Many of these objects were found in Roman rubbish pits, settlement sites or graves. Archaeologists have to decide what all this evidence means and what it tells them about Roman times.

These Roman shoes have survived because the leather they are made from has been preserved in wet ground.

6

ROMAN WRITING

The Romans left us accounts of their wars, plays, poems, recipe books and letters, amongst other writings. Only rarely do the original pieces of writing survive. However, we can still read Roman writings because many of them were copied out by monks in the medieval period.

The letter above has survived from Roman times. It was found at Hadrian's Wall and is a birthday party invitation. It was written on a very thin piece of wood (see page 20 for more on Roman writing materials).

STANDING STRUCTURES

In many places, Roman buildings have survived. Sometimes we can see the remains of whole towns, such as Pompeii, Italy, which was buried under volcanic ash in 79 CE.

This building is the Colosseum in Rome, Italy, a huge amphitheatre built for gladiator fights and spectacular shows.

ON THE FARM

Most people in the Roman Empire lived in the countryside and farmed the land. At harvest time, workers cut the grain crops using sickles, like this one (*right*). One part of this sickle is missing – the wooden handle. The metal blade has rusted over time.

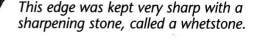

This edge was kept very sharp with a sharpening stone, called a whetstone.

FARMING

Many of the people who worked on the land were slaves, people taken prisoner in the wars across the Empire. They became the property of landowners who owned huge farm estates. These estates needed vast numbers of workers to grow crops and look after animals. However, not all the farms in the Roman Empire were large estates. There were also small farms, especially in Italy, owned by one family with the help of only one or two slaves.

MYSTERY OBJECT

If you lived in Roman times you might have seen this clever piece of equipment on a farm. What is it? (Answer on page 32.)

Farmworkers grab a handful of corn with one hand and slice through the stalks with the sickle.

SOME OF THE CROPS GROWN BY THE ROMANS

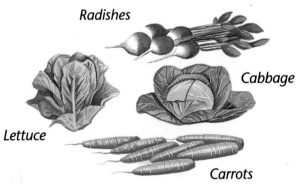

Radishes

Cabbage

Lettuce

Carrots

Oats

Barley

Pears

Dates

Apples

Cherries

Grapes

ON THE FARM

A big farm was called a *villa*, the word the Romans also used for a country or seaside house. Wealthy Romans owned one or more villas, as well as a town or city home where they lived most of the year. When the landowner wasn't there, a farm manager ran the farm. He grew a mixture of crops, as shown left, or concentrated on just one crop, like grapevines to make wine.

IN THE KITCHEN

Only wealthy Romans had proper kitchens at home. The cook used this *mortarium*, which we call a pestle (the grinder) and mortar (the bowl). It was like a food processor, and was used to grind up spices and mix up sauces by hand.

EATING OUT

In towns and cities, many people cooked over a brazier, a basic grill, or had no kitchen at all. So they bought hot food from street bars, or bread, olives, fruit and cheese from shops and stalls.

Here are some of the things for sale in shops and bars.

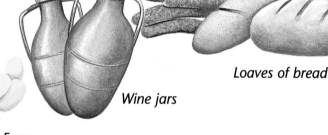

Sausages

Loaves of bread

Wine jars

Eggs

Olives

Bars, like the one shown here, sold a variety of snacks as well as drinks, such as watered-down wine and honey water. There were tables and benches to eat at inside, or you could stand at the bar. How much fish or meat you ate depended on your wealth.

Slaves did all the cooking in most wealthy homes.

MAKE YOUR OWN SWEETS

Here are two recipes from the Roman cookery writer, Apicius.

STUFFED DATES:

Remove the stones and fill the dates with nuts, pine kernels or pepper. Roll in salt and fry in honey.

HONEYED BREAD:

Soak pieces of bread in milk and then fry in olive oil. Pour over some honey before serving.

IN THE KITCHEN

Most food was cooked in pots stood over a charcoal fire. The cook prepared the main meal of the day in the afternoon. Wealthy Romans often asked friends to join them for dinner so the cook was kept busy producing fish and meat dishes, and strong-tasting sauces.

SOMEWHERE TO LIVE

Wealthy Romans filled their homes with comfortable furniture, like this couch, or sofa. Only the wooden frame survives today but historians have added material to show its full shape. It would have had a padded back, arms and seat, like the one opposite.

FLAT OR HOUSE?

Where you lived depended on whether you were rich or poor. In towns and cities, most people lived in flats while the poorest people lived in one-room homes. More wealthy people could afford a large flat or a town house, and maybe a country house on the farm.

IN THE GARDEN

Bigger houses were built around a square courtyard, open to the sky. Many had carefully laid out gardens. Here the family walked along paths, shaded by plants and trees and lined with flowers and herbs.

Grapevines

Parsley

Fennel

Mint

Bay tree

Fig tree

Apple tree

Cherry tree

A wealthy lady sits on her comfortable couch in the living room.

A drawing of a Roman mosaic found at Lullingstone, England.

WALLS AND FLOORS

Wealthy Romans liked well-decorated homes. They paid artists to paint pictures (murals) on the walls, and hung up painted wooden panels. Mosaic floors were popular, also. Craftsmen created pictures or patterns using thousands of coloured tiles stuck to the floor.

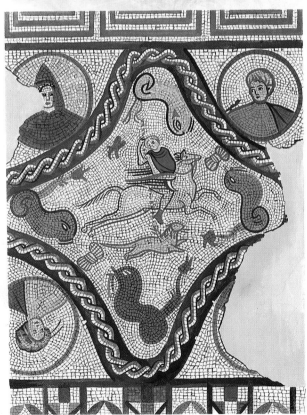

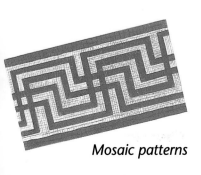

Mosaic patterns

WHAT SHALL I WEAR TODAY?

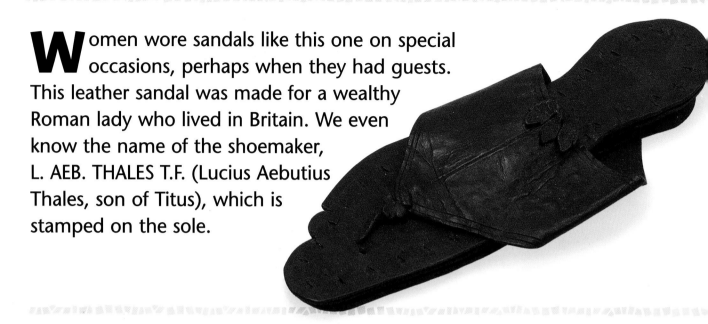

Women wore sandals like this one on special occasions, perhaps when they had guests. This leather sandal was made for a wealthy Roman lady who lived in Britain. We even know the name of the shoemaker, L. AEB. THALES T.F. (Lucius Aebutius Thales, son of Titus), which is stamped on the sole.

CLOTHES FOR ALL

Very few Roman clothes or shoes survive today as fabric and leather are quick to rot. We know how the Romans dressed from surviving paintings and statues.

Roman clothes showed what sort of person you were – rich or poor, slave or Roman citizen. Most people, including children, wore simple tunics made of wool or linen. Wealthy women wore a long dress over the top, called a *stola*. Their husbands could wear a *toga* if they were Roman citizens. Wool clothes or shawls kept people warm in cold weather.

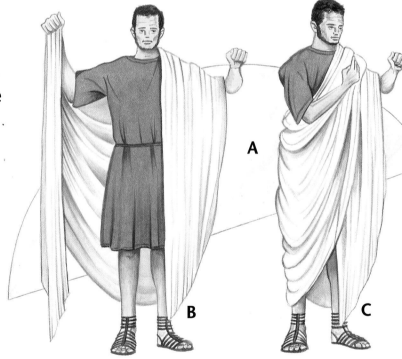

HOW TO TIE YOUR TOGA

The toga (**A**) was a semicircle of cloth. To put it on, the man had to drape one corner over his left shoulder until it reached his foot (**B**). He passed the other end under his right arm and across his left shoulder (**C**). It then had to be pinned and tucked to hold it in place.

*The slave wears a tunic,
while his master wears
a toga and his mistress a stola.*

JEWELLERY

Archaeologists have dug up many pieces of Roman jewellery. Earrings made from metal and precious stones were very popular. Women had matching necklaces, just like today. Men and women used brooches to hold their clothes together. Many people wore rings.

HAIRSTYLES

Many women wore elaborate hairstyles, held in place with pins. Some dyed their hair, while others wore wigs.

KEEPING CLEAN

F ew Romans had a bath at home, so they visited the public bathhouse (the baths) to get clean. There, a slave rubbed olive oil onto the bather's skin. In the heat of the baths, the bather sweated. Then the slave scraped the oil, sweat and dirt off the skin, using a *strigil* (*right*).

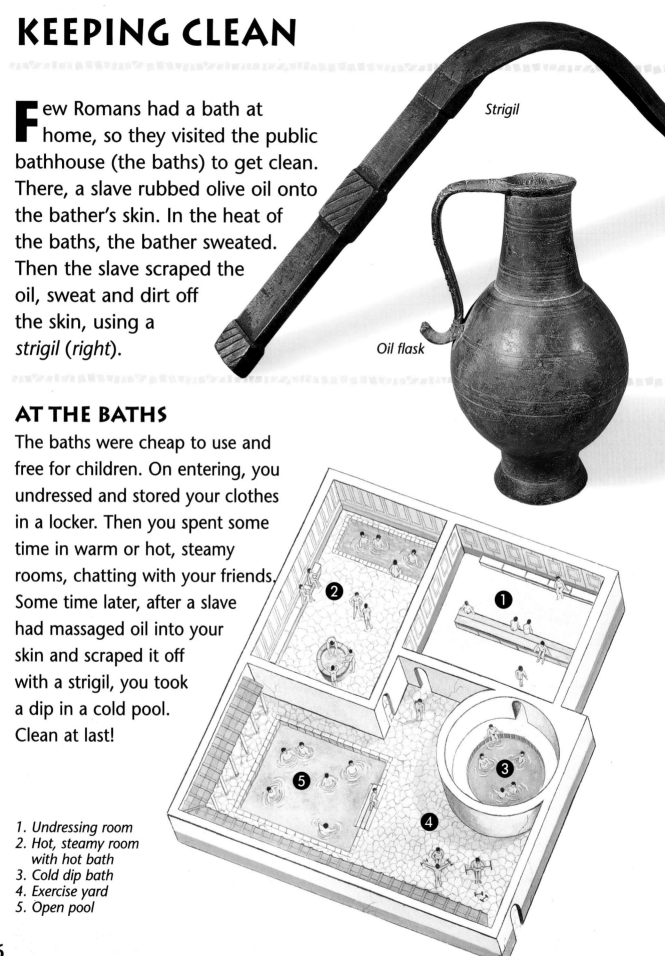

Strigil

Oil flask

AT THE BATHS

The baths were cheap to use and free for children. On entering, you undressed and stored your clothes in a locker. Then you spent some time in warm or hot, steamy rooms, chatting with your friends. Some time later, after a slave had massaged oil into your skin and scraped it off with a strigil, you took a dip in a cold pool. Clean at last!

1. *Undressing room*
2. *Hot, steamy room with hot bath*
3. *Cold dip bath*
4. *Exercise yard*
5. *Open pool*

HEATING THE BATHS

A large number of slaves worked at the baths, looking after the fire that heated the baths. This fire blasted hot air under the raised floors and behind the walls of the baths. The nearer to the fire, the hotter the room.

Men and women visited the baths at different times of day. The man at the front of this picture is having his skin scraped clean with a strigil.

MYSTERY
OBJECT

This little object is made of bronze. Each tool helped people get clean. Can you guess what it is?
(Answer on page 32.)

RELAXING

The Romans played sport, like catching games, in the exercise yard of the baths. They also enjoyed boardgames, using glass counters. Gambling with dice was another favourite pastime, or people sat chatting or eating snacks with friends.

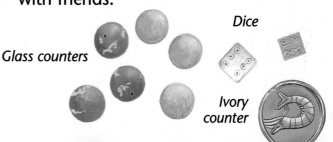

Glass counters

Dice

Ivory counter

GOING SHOPPING

Shopping was an important part of town life. This Roman tombstone gives us a picture of a butcher's shop. Waiting for her order, a woman sits with her shopping list on her lap. The butcher chops meat.

ROMAN SHOPS

Early in the morning, Roman shopkeepers removed the shutters from their shops. Now the shops were open to the street and open for business.

Most Roman shops produced their goods for sale in the shop. If you went to buy bread, for instance, you would see the baker grinding the flour, kneading the dough and baking the bread in the oven.

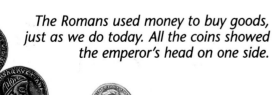

The Romans used money to buy goods, just as we do today. All the coins showed the emperor's head on one side.

Some shops had signs advertising their goods. This entire illustration shows a clothmaker's sign that can still be seen above a doorway in Pompeii, Italy. The small pictures at the bottom show wool being cleaned, woven into cloth and sold.

A busy Roman shopping street.

SOME OF THE GOODS FOR SALE ON A ROMAN SHOPPING STREET

Comb and mirror

Swan (to cook and eat)

Pillow

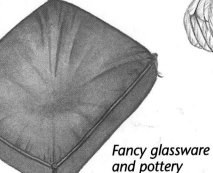

Fancy glassware and pottery

GOING SHOPPING

There were no supermarkets in Roman towns so shoppers had to move from shop to shop, gathering up what they needed. Many shopkeepers and craftspeople lived in rooms behind, or above, their shops.

There were also open-air markets where farmers sold fresh food. In addition, street-sellers sold goods, such as sausages, from trays carried on the head.

READING AND WRITING

Only the children of wealthier families learnt to read and write. To do so, they used a reusable writing tablet (*right*). There would have been a thick layer of wax inside the wooden frame. The Romans used the pointed object, called a *stylus*, to scratch letters in the wax. The flat end smoothed the wax over, ready to be used again.

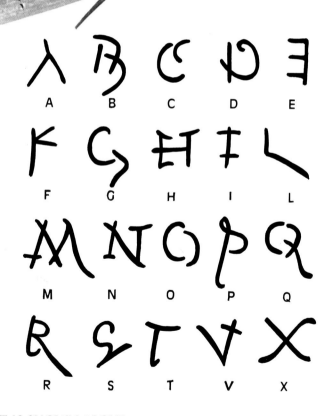

WRITING MATERIALS

Wax tablets were not the only writing material. The Romans also wrote in pen and ink on thin layers of wood or papyrus, a type of paper made from reeds. The most expensive writing material was vellum, a thin layer of animal skin.

This clock uses Roman numerals, rather than our number system. I = 1, V= 5 and X = 10.

THE ROMAN ALPHABET IS SHOWN ABOVE.
TRY USING IT TO WRITE A SENTENCE LIKE THE ONE BELOW.

READ ALL ABOUT THE ROMANS

CAN YOU READ WHAT IT SAYS?

School was usually a room in the teacher's house, or a rented room in the town.

SCHOOL

There was no free education in Roman times. The sons, and a few of the daughters, of wealthier families started school at the age of seven. They learnt to read and write Latin, and to do some maths. At the age of eleven, pupils went to secondary school where they studied literature, history, maths and astronomy.

WRITERS

Homer (born c.725 BCE) wrote two long poems in Greek – the *Iliad* and the *Odyssey*, that were studied in Roman times.
Virgil (born 70 BCE) wrote the *Aeneid*, amongst other poems.
Cicero (born 106 BCE) was a Roman politician. Pupils studied his speeches.
Julius Caesar (born 100 BCE) wrote accounts of his military campaigns.
Seneca (born c.4 BCE) wrote many books about how Romans should live their lives.

| Homer | Virgil | Cicero | Julius Caesar | Seneca |

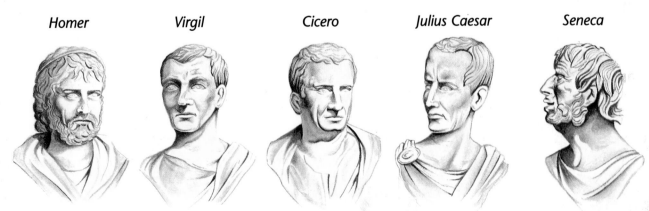

MAKING JOURNEYS

The Romans built roads all across their empire. They did not have signposts but they did have milestones, like this one from North Wales. Like other Roman milestones, it gives the number of miles from a place, in this case 8 (VIII) miles from Kanovium. The letters and numbers were painted with bright colours to make them stand out.

THE NEED FOR ROADS

You can see from the map on pages 4 and 5 just how big the Roman Empire was. Many people travelled across the Empire. The army needed to reach trouble spots, merchants wanted to transport goods, and government officials needed to travel to keep control of the Empire.

When the Romans invaded new lands, their army built roads. After that, it was up to the local government to keep them in good repair and to build new ones.

The Romans built their roads so well that many survive today.

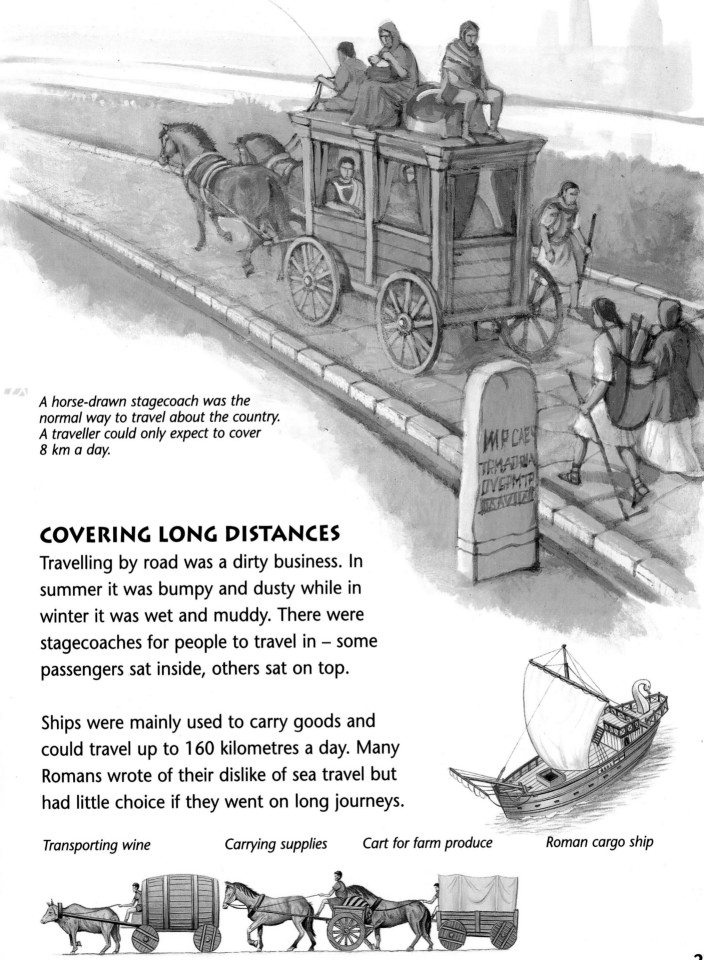

A horse-drawn stagecoach was the normal way to travel about the country. A traveller could only expect to cover 8 km a day.

COVERING LONG DISTANCES

Travelling by road was a dirty business. In summer it was bumpy and dusty while in winter it was wet and muddy. There were stagecoaches for people to travel in – some passengers sat inside, others sat on top.

Ships were mainly used to carry goods and could travel up to 160 kilometres a day. Many Romans wrote of their dislike of sea travel but had little choice if they went on long journeys.

Transporting wine   *Carrying supplies*   *Cart for farm produce*   *Roman cargo ship*

GOING TO A SHOW

Romans who lived in towns could choose from a variety of shows for their entertainment. This decorated pot (*right*) shows a gladiator fight, a popular show. The gladiators' names are written above them – Memnon (*left*) and Valentinus (*right*). Valentinus is holding up one finger, a sign that he is asking for mercy from Memnon.

ROMAN ENTERTAINMENT

The Romans built grand buildings for entertainment. Wealthy Roman politicians or leaders paid for many of the shows, to gain public support. Thousands attended – perhaps 20,000 to watch a play, 50,000 to watch gladiator fights and 200,000 to watch chariot races.

CHARIOTEERS

At the races, charioteers drove chariots pulled by four horses. They competed in teams, each one represented by a different colour – the Reds, the Blues, the Greens and the Whites. Skilled charioteers became wealthy but it was a dangerous sport with many deaths.

*Gladiators usually fought
to the death. Sometimes the
audience spared the life of the loser.*

*A Roman mosaic shows actors
preparing for a performance.*

MUSIC AND THEATRE

There were plenty of opportunities for Romans to watch plays at the theatre. The actors wore face masks to help their voices reach to the back of the huge open-air theatres. The type of mask and the costume also helped the audience understand the story. Musicians performed music as part of the play but gave concerts also, often in small theatres called *odeons*.

IN THE ARMY

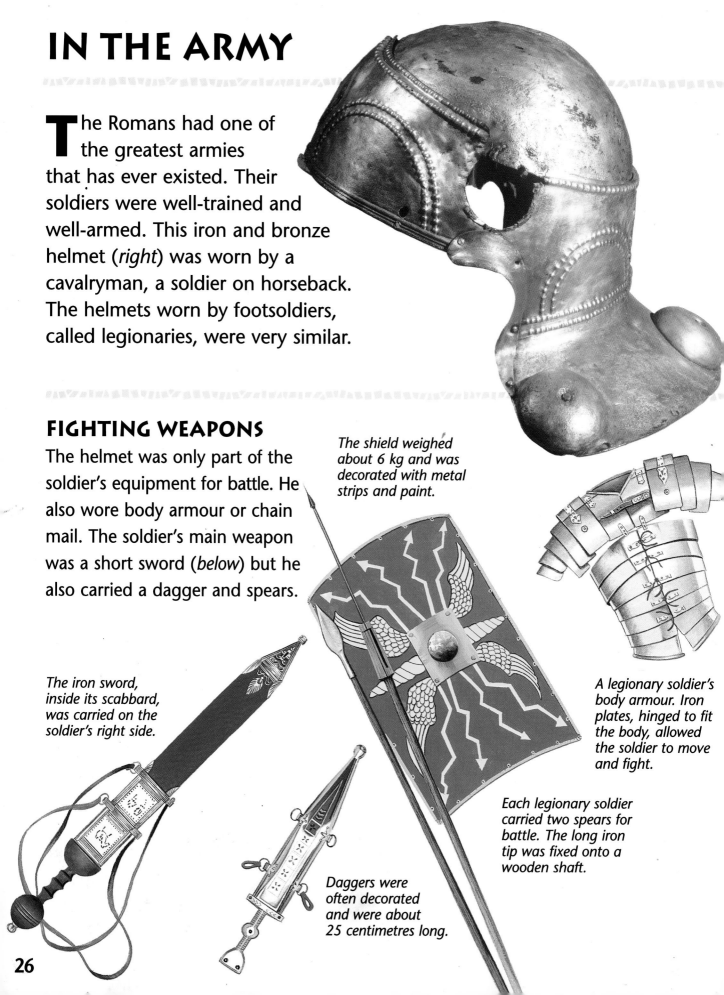

The Romans had one of the greatest armies that has ever existed. Their soldiers were well-trained and well-armed. This iron and bronze helmet (*right*) was worn by a cavalryman, a soldier on horseback. The helmets worn by footsoldiers, called legionaries, were very similar.

FIGHTING WEAPONS

The helmet was only part of the soldier's equipment for battle. He also wore body armour or chain mail. The soldier's main weapon was a short sword (*below*) but he also carried a dagger and spears.

The shield weighed about 6 kg and was decorated with metal strips and paint.

The iron sword, inside its scabbard, was carried on the soldier's right side.

A legionary soldier's body armour. Iron plates, hinged to fit the body, allowed the soldier to move and fight.

Each legionary soldier carried two spears for battle. The long iron tip was fixed onto a wooden shaft.

Daggers were often decorated and were about 25 centimetres long.

Guards kept watch at the fort's four gates,
and from the watch towers.

SOLDIERS OF RANK

As in any army, there were Roman
soldiers of different rank and soldiers
for particular jobs.

Legionary   *Cavalryman*   *Standard bearer*

Centurian   *Auxiliary*

THE FORT

All over the Empire, the Romans built
forts to house the army. Inside each
fort, the soldiers lived in long buildings
divided into at least ten pairs of rooms.
Each pair of rooms housed eight men –
one room had bunkbeds while the
other room was for cooking and
storing equipment. When they were on
the move, soldiers made camps at
night and slept in tents.

BUILDERS AND ENGINEERS

The Romans were skilled builders and engineers. Many of their buildings survive today, such as the Pont du Gard (*right*). It carried an aqueduct (water channel) which ran for over 50 km in all and carried 20,000 tonnes of water a day to the people of Nîmes, France.

Colourful mosaics on the floors of Roman houses give us pictures of scenes from everyday life. Here the grape harvest is being collected into...

ROMAN BUILDERS

The Romans built public buildings, like baths, theatres and temples, as well as roads, bridges and blocks of flats. They discovered how to make concrete out of volcanic rocks and rubble. This allowed them to build even bigger buildings as concrete is not as heavy as stone.

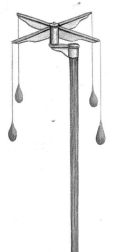

The weights hanging down from the groma held the strings straight.

THE GROMA

The groma *(below)* was used by a surveyor to mark out straight lines in building projects. Using the groma, the Romans built extremely straight roads.

A Roman crane lifts blocks of stone for the bridge.

BUILDING THE BRIDGE

The Pont du Gard was built during the reign of Emperor Claudius (27 BCE–14 CE) to carry the aqueduct across a river. Roman engineers had a variety of tools and machines to help them, including the crane above. People powered the crane by walking inside the wheel, or treadmill. It lifted heavy blocks of stone, cut to the right size by skilled workers.

Many streets had fountains and water troughs, filled by underground pipes. People fetched water for use at home.

WORSHIPPING THE GODS

Religion was an important part of life, and death. This Roman tombstone shows the funeral feast of Julia Velva, who lies surrounded by her family. The Romans believed it was extremely important to mourn people properly in order to send them on their journey to the afterlife, a place they called Hades.

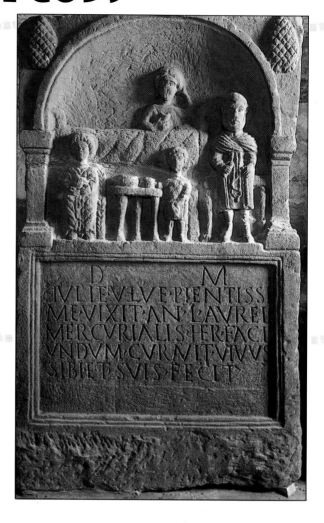

WORSHIP AT HOME AND IN THE TEMPLE

Most Roman families made offerings to the household gods at small altars in the home. They also worshipped the other gods at temples and shrines.

Household altar

GODS AND GODDESSES

For most of the Roman period, the Romans worshipped a large number of gods and goddesses. People believed that each god or goddess could help them in a different way. Towards the end of the Roman Empire, Christianity became the official religion.

Minerva was the goddess of wisdom, crafts, trades and industry. She is often shown in armour.

The family paid actors and musicians to lead the funeral procession of their loved one.

FUNERALS

At different times in the Roman period, people were either cremated or buried. After an elaborate funeral, people carried the ashes or body to the cemetery, a place just outside the town walls, along the roadside.

Jupiter was the god of the sky and king of all the gods. He was called "the greatest and the best".

Apollo was a Greek god worshipped by the Romans. They believed he could reveal the future.

Mithras was originally a Persian god. Soldiers and merchants particularly liked his bravery.

Neptune was the god of water and the sea. He is usually shown with a pronged spear.

INDEX

ANSWERS TO MYSTERY OBJECT BOXES

Page 8: This is a farm machine, called a *vallus*. The donkey pushed the machine, with its rotating blades, into the crop. The blades cut the corn, which fell into the scoop.

Page 17: This is a personal grooming set. The top tool was used to scoop out ear wax, the middle one to clean nails and the last one is a pair of tweezers to remove splinters.